Animals Eat **WHAT?!**

GARBAGE and TRASH

Holly Duhig

Lerner Publications ◆ Minneapolis

First American edition published in 2020 by Lerner Publishing Group, Inc.

© 2019 Booklife Publishing
This edition is published by arrangement with Booklife Publishing.
All rights reserved.

Editor: Kirsty Holmes
Design: Jasmine Porter

Lerner Publications Company
An imprint of Lerner Publishing Group, Inc.
241 First Avenue North
Minneapolis, MN 55401 USA

For reading levels and more information, look up this title at www.lernerbooks.com.

Main body text set in VAG Rounded Std. Typeface provided by Adobe Systems.

Photo credits:
Images are courtesy of Shutterstock.com, with thanks to Getty Images, Thinkstock Photo, and iStockphoto. Freddy the Fly: Natthapon Boochagorn & Roi and Roi. Front cover: Rvector, Hari Syahputra, NotionPic, Daria Riabets, Pixsooz. 2: Top Vector Studio. 5: Eric Isselee, Aedka Studio, Iakov Filimonov. 6: Top Vector Studio. 7: neenawat khenyothaa. 8: PunkbarbyO. 9: Grimgram. 10: Adam Dobias. 11: BlueRingMedia, Sonsedska Yuliia. 12: Janis Susa. 13: Grandpa. 14: Nila Newsom. 15: Anna Kucherova, Martin Mecnarowski. 16: Akulinina. 17: ByEmo, Eduard Radu. 18: Stefan foto video. 19: Hesitantpatcha. 20: Gribov Andrei Aleksandrovich. 21: Amelia Martin. 22: By Rich Carey. 23: EniaB.

Library of Congress Cataloging-in-Publication Data

Names: Duhig, Holly, author.
Title: Garbage and trash / Holly Duhig.
Description: Minneapolis : Lerner Publications, 2020. | Series: Animals eat what? | Includes index. | Audience: Ages 6–10 | Audience: Grades 2–3 | Summary: "Do animals really eat garbage and trash? They sure do! Full-color photography and funny facts will engage young readers in learning about the biological processes of living things"— Provided by publisher.
Identifiers: LCCN 2019028060 (print) | LCCN 2019028061 (ebook) | ISBN 9781541579330 (library binding) | ISBN 9781541587052 (paperback) | ISBN 9781541582590 (ebook)
Subjects: LCSH: Scavengers (Zoology)—Juvenile literature. | Animals—Food—Juvenile literature.
Classification: LCC QL756.5 .D844 2020 (print) | LCC QL756.5 (ebook) | DDC 591.5/3—dc23

LC record available at https://lccn.loc.gov/2019028060
LC ebook record available at https://lccn.loc.gov/2019028061

Manufactured in the United States of America
1-47215-47920-7/16/2019

Contents

WORDS THAT LOOK LIKE <u>THIS</u> CAN BE FOUND IN THE GLOSSARY ON PAGE 24.

Animals Eat What?!

All animals need to eat food to stay alive. However, some animals have different ideas about what counts as "food."

IT IS I, FREDDY THE FLY, WORLD-FAMOUS CRITIC OF <u>UNUSUAL</u> FOOD!

I CAN'T WAIT TO TRY SOME OF THE DELICIOUS DISHES THE ANIMAL KINGDOM HAS TO OFFER. FLIES AREN'T PICKY EATERS!

LEECHES DRINK BLOOD.

HYENAS MUNCH ON BONES.

CHIMPS EAT THEIR OWN POOP.

Gourmet Garbage

You might not be interested in the leftovers hiding in your neighborhood garbage bins, but for many animals, trash cans are full of <u>nutritious</u> snacks. Some animals depend on the things we throw away to stay alive.

Animals that eat garbage and trash instead of hunting for food are called scavengers. Although this might sound lazy, scavengers do a great job of cleaning up after humans!

FLIES ARE VERY GOOD SCAVENGERS. DON'T SWAT US AWAY!

Rubbish Rummagers

Rats are one of the main scavengers in cities. Rats like to live in <u>urban</u> areas because there are lots of cafés and restaurants with dumpsters they can call home. A big city like New York has about two million rats!

Because of their habit of moving into houses and restaurants, rats are seen as pests. They can easily nibble through garbage bags and make a big mess.

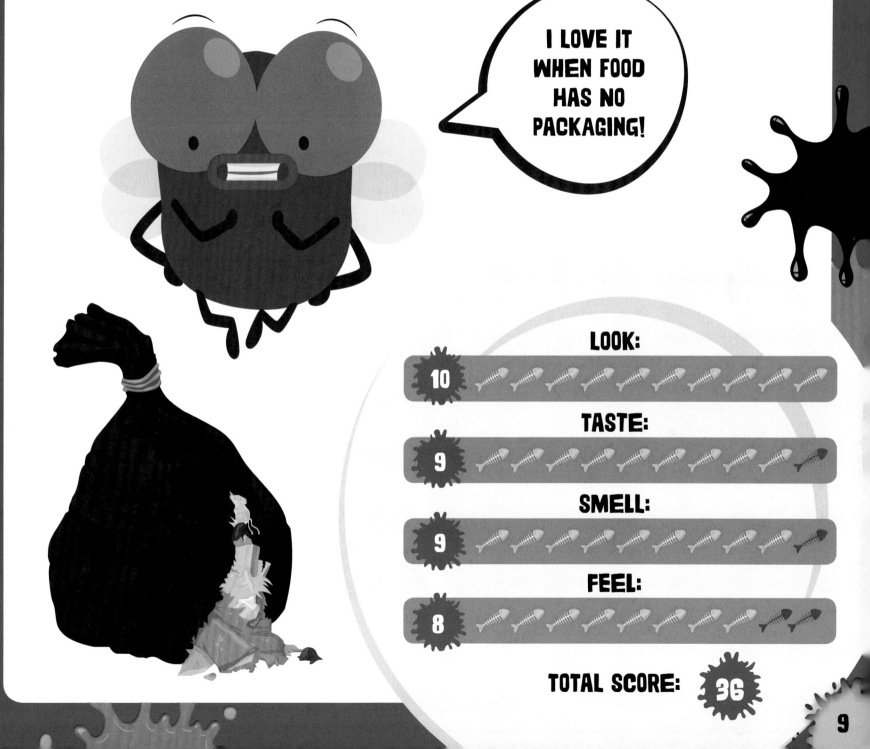

I LOVE IT WHEN FOOD HAS NO PACKAGING!

LOOK:
10

TASTE:
9

SMELL:
9

FEEL:
8

TOTAL SCORE: 36

Dumpster Divers

Raccoons are well-known for dumpster diving. They are omnivores. This means they eat both meat and plants. In the wild, raccoons will eat anything from fruits and nuts to insects and dead animals.

RACCOONS HAVE HAND-LIKE PAWS THAT ARE VERY GOOD AT OPENING TRASH CAN LIDS.

LOOK:

10

TASTE:

4

SMELL:

1

FEEL:

4

TOTAL SCORE: 19

THIS MEAL MIGHT BE STOLEN, BUT I HAPPEN TO LOVE LEFTOVERS.

However, like rats, raccoons are often seen as pests because of how much they dig through trash. Raccoons have even been known to sneak into people's houses to eat out of their garbage cans!

Swill-Eating Swine

Pigs are not picky eaters! Like raccoons, they are omnivores and will eat almost anything. In the past, pig farmers would use kitchen waste to feed to their pigs. This waste was called pig swill and was kept in swill bins.

In the United Kingdom during World War II, it wasn't just farmers collecting scraps and leftovers. Everybody was asked to put their kitchen waste in special bins. These bins were collected, and their contents were used to make pig food.

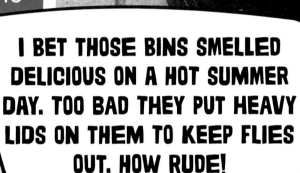

I BET THOSE BINS SMELLED DELICIOUS ON A HOT SUMMER DAY. TOO BAD THEY PUT HEAVY LIDS ON THEM TO KEEP FLIES OUT. HOW RUDE!

LOOK:
10

TASTE:
10

SMELL:
10

FEEL:
10

TOTAL SCORE: 40

Leftovers for Langurs

In Jodhpur, India, langur monkeys rule the streets. They live in the city alongside humans. They are very good at stealing and scavenging food that people throw away.

Langur monkeys would sometimes steal food from people's houses or market stalls. To stop this, people began putting out food for the monkeys in the temple gardens.

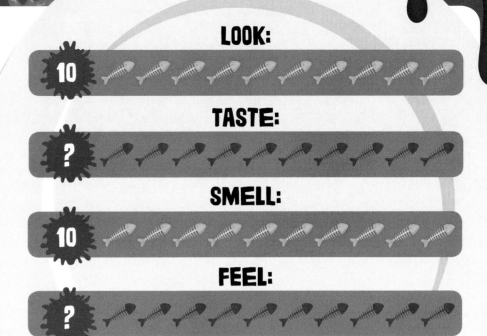

LOOK: 10

TASTE: ?

SMELL: 10

FEEL: ?

TOTAL SCORE: 20

WHEN THE LANGURS WANT LEFTOVERS, THEY CAN HEAD TO THE TEMPLE INSTEAD OF STEALING. HEY! THOSE ARE MINE!

Litter Pickers

Seagulls are fish-eating birds that usually live near the ocean. However, they will live farther <u>inland</u> if there's grub up for grabs.

Seagulls love eating garbage so much that many live at landfills.

Landfills are places where garbage is buried in a deep hole in the ground. However, as the garbage slowly breaks down, it releases harmful <u>chemicals</u>. The food that seagulls eat may contain these chemicals. This can be very bad for the birds.

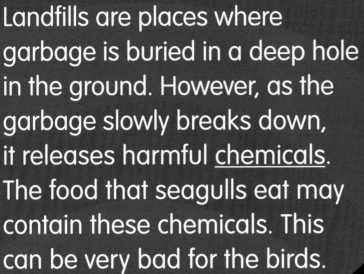

I RECENTLY VACATIONED AT A LANDFILL IN THE SOUTH OF FRANCE. FANTASTIC FOOD!

LOOK:
6

TASTE:
8

SMELL:
8

FEEL:
9

TOTAL SCORE: 31

Ants in the Big Apple

Ants live on every <u>continent</u> on earth except for Antarctica. They are very good at finding food and litter that people throw away. Cities are perfect places for ants. In New York City, there are forty-two different <u>species</u> of ant!

People don't like ants very much, but they are very helpful to our cities. Ants eat a lot of thrown-away food that could attract rats. Rats can carry germs that are dangerous to humans.

I LOVE OLD APPLE CORES TOO!

LOOK:
3

TASTE:
9

SMELL:
7

FEEL:
10

TOTAL SCORE: 29

Bin-Busting Bears

SLUUURP!

Bears are scavengers, and they will often eat animals that have already died. However, bears that live in parks see trash cans as an even better source of food.

BEAR-PROOF BIN

WHY DOES EVERYONE WANT TO STOP ME FROM EATING TODAY? I'M STARVING!

LOOK:

0

TASTE:

0

SMELL:

0

FEEL:

0

TOTAL SCORE: 0

There are lots of bears in Yellowstone National Park. When nobody is looking, they will dig through garbage cans that are used by <u>tourists</u>. To stop this from happening, people started to design bear-proof bins. The bears tested them themselves!

Do You Eat Trash?

Almost nine million tons of plastic end up in the ocean every year. Sea creatures, including turtles and fish, end up eating this plastic.

These plastics end up on our dinner plates! In fact, at markets in Indonesia and California, one in every four fish had plastic in their guts. This means that, not only are fish eating our trash, but we are too!

WE CAN HELP PROTECT SEA CREATURES BY USING REUSABLE BAGS INSTEAD OF PLASTIC ONES.

PLASTIC IS THE ONLY THING I WON'T EAT. BLEUGH!

LOOK:

0

TASTE:

0

SMELL:

0

FEEL:

0

TOTAL SCORE: 0

Glossary

CHEMICALS	substances that materials are made from
CONTINENT	a very large area of land, such as Africa or Europe, that is made up of many countries
CRITIC	someone whose job it is to judge something, such as food
INLAND	away from the coast
NUTRITIOUS	full of the natural substances that plants and animals need to grow and stay healthy
SPECIES	a group of very similar animals or plants
TOURISTS	people who are visiting a place for fun
URBAN	relating to a town or city

Index